Game Changer

Game Changer

Ian Tudor

Contents

Introduction

CONGRATULATIONS ON DISCOVERING GAME CHANGER, this book is written specifically for elite level athletes that desire total victory over their competitors. If your goal is first place, then this concise guide will get you there FAST. By simply adopting the methods in this book, you will literally blow away the competition.

The premise of this powerful little book is to bring together the most advanced, cutting-edge performance enhancement practices and deliver them directly and easily to you.

The pioneers of high performance have provided the basis of this guide to victory. By reading their remarkable achievements and employing their methods you can emulate their success within your own chosen sport. From their personal stories to the science behind their methodology, you will learn exactly how to amplify your performance to peak, faster and more efficiently than any other course of action. By simply following the steps laid out in each chapter, your sporting success is, for the most part, guaranteed.

Allow this book to fascinate and amaze you as you realize how to maximize the full potential of the human body.

I wish you the greatest success imaginable in your

quest to become the best you can be, and furthermore, I grant you the knowledge to manifest what you imagine into being with this special little book.

Happy reading from the author, Ian Tudor

CHAPTER ONE

The Wim Hof Method

W H A T   I S   T H E   W I M   H O F   M E T H O D ?

A combination of three disciplines, the Wim Hof Method produces record-breaking and extraordinary increases in performance and produces faster results. It is completely verified and scientifically proven to work time and again.

This method requires no equipment, no long training period and no specialised coaching. Simply practising the specific disciplines can transform an athlete's level of performance from average to peak in just a few days.

The pioneer of this method is a man called Wim Hof, from the Netherlands. Widely known as "The Ice Man" for his ability to withstand extreme cold, his super human feats have included:

1. Exposing his bare skin to a large mass of ice for three hours with no ill effects

2. Running a half marathon in Finland, bare footed and wearing only shorts in temperatures of minus 20 degrees centigrade

3. Trekking up Mount Everest to the area known as "The Death Zone" wearing only boots, shorts and a t-shirt

As well as undertaking these remarkable feats, Wim Hof has undertaken numerous medical studies, his vital signs and blood monitored by doctors, while undertaking exercise in a controlled laboratory setting. The most notable study being when he agreed to be injected with an endotoxin known to attack the endocrine system. This endotoxin causes extreme nausea and vomiting lasting for a minimum of six hours with subjects exposed to the endotoxin normally requiring hospitalisation.

After just ten minutes of being injected, Wim Hof had stabilised himself, and his vital signs and blood were at completely normal levels. The doctors monitoring him were astounded at what they were witnessing, as this type of recovery had never been recorded before.

Here was a person able to consciously control their endocrine system and their autonomic nervous system. Wim Hof had managed to reverse everything that the scientific community and medical journals believed they knew about human physiology.

Wim Hof was hailed as a miracle of human extremes. A unique, 'one off' human being.

Was it that he was a genetic freak, pre-disposed to having this innate and incredible physical gift?

You can imagine how stunned the doctors were when Wim Hof disclosed to them that it was, in fact, the contrary. He was not unique. He could, in fact, teach other people his incredible power.

This excited the doctors no end. They agreed that they would use test subjects to repeat the endotoxin experiment to confirm whether or not, this bold claim by Wim

Hof could actually be proven.

If Wim Hof could produce the same results again, this time with a set of test subjects, it would be a breakthrough in scientific understanding, proving beyond a shadow of a doubt that the human body held a much greater physical capacity for endurance and recovery than ever previously known. Conventional medical and physiological books on the human body would have to be re-written and revised.

THE EXPERIMENT

Test subjects were split into two groups.

One group would be injected with the endotoxin, but without any training from Wim Hof.

The other group would be injected at the same time, but only after Wim Hof's training and guidance.

Wim Hof began working with his group. Starting with simple breathing exercises, he demonstrated to the volunteers how to take in a deep breath and relax while releasing only around one tenth of air on the exhale.

He asked them to repeat this, for a total of thirty breaths.

This meant that they were taking in more air than they were exhaling. By exhaling only a little breath at a time it meant they were able to inhale air even deeper into their lungs on the next breath.

He explained to the doctors and his subjects that the body has a much higher capacity to store oxygen than imagined. We only use a tiny fraction of this capacity in normal shallow breathing, and so by training the breath and lungs in this way, we can naturally increase overall capacity.

On breath number thirty, Wim Hof told his group to return to normal breathing.

Next, he asked them to inhale and see how long they could hold a single breath. The volunteers and doctors were astounded. They were, each and every one, able to hold a breath for over a minute, much longer than before. This was a direct result of the previous breathing exercise enabling them to increase their capacity to hold and store oxygen.

The group were told to repeat several cycles. Taking thirty deep breaths, relaxing briefly between each breath, and letting a little air exhale before taking the next deep breath.

After repeating five breathing cycles of thirty, the group were instructed to practice the same technique at home whilst taking a cold shower.

They were asked to relax, take in one breath, hold, and repeat for approximately three minutes, releasing the breath when required. The goal, he explained, was to concentrate and focus the mind on not allowing the body to gasp for air or tense up.

The method of taking a cold shower served two key purposes to Wim Hof's method.

Firstly, it was a practice in focusing the mind away from the cold, thereby increasing overall mental focus.

Secondly, the exercise was physically conditioning the cardio vascular system (namely the veins and arteries) to work more efficiently by using the cold stimuli.

Although the subjects tensed and gasped for air on the first or second attempt of the exercise, they continued to practice the breathing protocol over a couple of days, along with short, periodic cold showers. They soon discovered that they were able to withstand the cold showers and ice bathing for increasingly extended periods of time without the need to gasp or tense up.

After a while, they were able to exercise in shorts under very cold conditions, without feeling any untoward effects.

Wim Hof was pleased with the progress his new students had made. However, he was conscious of the upcoming medical experiment involving the endotoxin.

Would his group be capable of achieving what he had achieved?

He decided the best plan was to over-prepare his students, rather than risk failure. The training continued in freezing conditions, and group confidence grew as well as ability. The endurance increased with training, until it got to the point that Wim Hof finally decided his students were ready for one final, testing challenge.

He lead the group up a mountain on the Czech border, the group dressed only in shorts and boots, without the normal protective gear usually needed for such an expedition.

He already knew from progress made by the group that the expedition was within their sphere of competence, but he wondered if they would all have the confidence to achieve it.

They proceeded up the snow-covered mountain with relative ease. All were bare chested, wearing only boots and shorts. Despite the extreme cold, everyone in the group was achieving well, following the breathing method practised in training. As they neared the summit, temperatures were coming in at -12 degrees centigrade.

Suddenly, a group of special forces patrolling the border showed up. Wim Hof describes the special forces unit as, "dressed up like ninjas," wearing heavy duty, specialist gear designed for extreme cold.

The special forces patrol was astounded at the sight of bare chested explorers walking in freezing conditions, seemingly enjoying themselves, even laughing and joking amongst themselves! It was for them, a bizarre, almost supernatural scene to behold. After the initial surprise of encountering each other, greetings were exchanged and Wim Hof's group began taking selfies with the, by now, friendly and admiring special forces patrol, who were both intrigued and amazed at this unique encounter.

Wim Hof now knew that his students were fully pre-pared for the test. He was immensely proud of what the group had achieved.

The day of the test arrived Would Wim Hof's group succeed or fail? Or would some and not all, pass the test?

It was time to find out.

The scientists took Wim Hof's group, along with the non-trained test group, and tested them under the same conditions and parameters as the original experiment on Wim Hof.

Both groups were injected with the endotoxin. Now they could only wait. This was the moment of truth.

The experiment began. Both test groups became nauseated as expected. The non-trained group deteriorated into fever and vomiting, all requiring hospitalization, in order to recover.

On the other hand, after only a few minutes, Wim Hof's trained group began to moderate themselves. Within a short space of time, they were completely stable, displaying normal blood and vital signs.

The experiment was nothing short of a massive success.

Wim Hof had been proved right, in both his practice and theory. He was not a genetic freak, or a one-of-a-kind human being, possessing a gift. He was a pioneer who had discovered a scientific method to increase the human body's capacity to hold and store oxygen. He had also found a way to enable the human body to push far beyond all or any limitations previously described as "fixed"....

Thus, the Wim Hof method was born.

How to Perform the Wim Hof Method, Step by Step

Lie down on a sofa or bed and take a few minutes to relax in preparation for the upcoming breathing protocol. The reason for taking these short few minutes to relax is because the body can take in and store substantially more oxygen when in a relaxed state.

Go ahead and take a few minutes until you feel relaxed and comfortable.

Now let us begin.

1. Take a deep breath into the lungs, as deep as possible, either through the mouth or the nose, as you prefer, attempting to fully inflate the lungs. As you feel the urge to exhale, keep calm and only exhale a minimal amount of air in order to relax your diaphragm in readiness to inhale another deep breath.

Hold the thought in your mind that you are drawing in ten litres of air, and only exhaling one litre of air – a ratio of ten : one. This will help you focus more clearly on the purpose of the breathing protocol.

The idea is to get in a much greater volume of air than you exhale, pushing oxygen deep into the blood for storage before breathing out only just enough to relax, before drawing in another deep breath, further pushing more oxygen into the blood.

In short, a deep powerful breath in, followed by a small breath out.

Repeat this thirty times with no pauses in between.

Then on breath number thirty, hold the air in your lungs before breathing out and relaxing.

This total of thirty breaths is one full cycle of breathing and the cycle is now complete.

Take a minute or two before starting another cycle of thirty. Overall, you will complete a total of three cycles of thirty.

Now that you have saturated your blood with oxygen, you may feel a little light headed. This is perfectly normal. You will also feel an overwhelming feeling of well-being.

2. Now take one deep breath and hold. As you hold, step into a cold shower, attempting neither to gasp or shiver.

This will be difficult on your first attempt. However, take note, simply, of the amount of times you do gasp or shiver and try to improve slightly for the next attempt.

You should aim for a total of three minutes under the cold shower and continue taking in one deep breath at a time, holding before slowly exhaling.

It is crucially important that you relax as much as possible and allow your mind to transcend above and beyond the cold. This can be done by focusing on controlling your breathing, which will prevent you becoming overwhelmed by the cold sensation of the water.

Use of a beep timer is recommended, which can be set to beep every thirty seconds (or every minute as you prefer). This makes it easier to monitor your three-minute time frame.

The breathing control and focusing of the mind is key

to this step. Your aim is to train the mind and body to work in a state of unison, facilitating complete harmony.

After three minutes, exit the shower and towel dry.

Your goal with the three-minute cold shower, as stated before, is to eliminate any gasping or shivering or tensing of the body. With practice, this can be achieved after only a couple of days. You should by then be able to enter the cold shower and stand completely relaxed, with the mind projected away from the cold with complete control of your breathing. Upon achieving this you will feel both invigorated and energised with a greater capacity of mental focus.

Congratulations – YOU DID IT!

This should be considered the conditioning phase of the method. It will give you a form of mental tool kit that you can use at any time as the challenges on the body gradually increase.

ICE BATH

In this session, you are going to substitute the three-minute cold shower with an ice bath.

Again, using exactly the same method above, aim for a target of three minutes. Ice can be taken from the freezer and placed into a bath tub that filled with water. Allow fifteen minutes for the water to cool. As stated above, you can complete three breathing cycles before taking in one longer breath.

Submerge into the ice bath up to neck level, exhale and inhale normally whilst focusing the mind away from the cold stimuli. Remember to take note of the amount of times you gasp or tense before improving these statistics the next time.

It is good to be aware that this type of focus training actually increases the body's ability to hold and maintain its core temperature. You may begin to feel warm or even hot whilst submerged in the ice bath. This is perfectly normal and demonstrates the adaptation of your cardio-vascular system.

You are physically and mentally becoming stronger and more efficient at dealing with the cold.

Once again, this method should be viewed, primarily, as a focusing and sharpening of the mind's ability to relax, become still, and project away from the cold stimuli. You are essentially training your mind, which in turn leads to a cascade of physiological improvements within the body.

Everything begins within the mind…

All of what has been described above is the basic core foundation of the Wim Hof Method. Of course, the challenges will change slightly, as well as gradually increase over time. Yet the basic technique used remains unchanged, a technique that has universal application for an elite athlete, from competition to recuperation.

Your role as an elite athlete is to practice this method daily until it is locked into your psyche and you can access it during competition, being able to deliver peak mental clarity and focus whenever the need arises.

Science Behind the Wim Hof Method

1. Every cell within the human body requires oxygen to

function properly. The mitochondria require oxygen in order to maintain health within the cells. By increasing the amount of oxygen in the blood using the Wim Hof Method, the mitochondria vastly improved its ability to increase vitality on a cellular level.

2. Acidity in the blood increases when performing intense physical activity, as well as when the body is under other miscellaneous forms of stress. This acidity has a negative effect on physical and mental performance. By working through the breathing cycles, this acidic state can be rapidly reduced to PH neutral, which in turn facilitates peak performance.

This can be demonstrated easily at home with the use of PH strips. Urinating onto a PH strip shows your blood PH levels, by changing colour. Yellow indicates that that the blood is acidic, and green/blue shows a neutral PH level.

After exercise, urinating on one of these strips will usually cause it to turn yellow, a sign of acidity in the blood. Perform just a few cycles of the Wim Hof Breathing Method, however and repeat the test You will find that it immediately turns green/blue. This indicates that the blood has been brought into the optimum neutral PH range.

This highlights a speedy turn-around in recovery from physical activity, which is invaluable to the elite athlete.

Maintaining blood alkalinity is key to any form of physical or mental performance either in training or competition. For you, it is the difference between being a runner up and a winner.

The muscles are continually producing lactic acid in any type of endurance event, and it is important to get these levels down. Significant reductions can be made by any athlete who has undergone the breathing and cold stimuli of the Wim Hof Method prior to these physical events. Undertaking this method enables you to control the internal mechanisms of your own body on a physio-logical level.

By doing this, you will be in direct contrast to a com-petitor who has not prepared using this method and has no concept of how to consciously control the inner physiological processes within their body during competition.

In short – a Wim Hof athlete going into competition against a non-Wim Hof athlete has a 35% competitive advantage. An unquestionably huge opportunity!

3. The mental focusing of the mind while submerged in an ice bath also plays a vital role, as it programmes the body to override the body's natural response of gasping or shivering. This means that stress hormones such as cortisol, are brought under control.

Being able to control your body and hormones whilst training and competing means you can go physically harder and longer. All this combined with having a greater level of mental focus due to the projecting of the mind away from the cold stimuli whilst submerged in the ice bath.

The body could be best described after preparing with this method as 'tempered'. You are now perfectly ready for high-performance by conditioning a vast array of physiological and mental processes. Just using this simple method, you will experience high levels of control over the body. In essence, unifying the mind and body connection.

Case Study

Alister Overeem is a highly decorated mixed martial artist, competing in the UFC as well as many other prestigious MMA tournaments.

He boasts a long list of victories over other elite level MMA champions.

Originally from the Netherlands, Alistair has a notable MMA pedigree. He had been trained by Bas Ruten, widely recognised as one of the greatest MMA fighters ever to grace the octagon.

Alister is characterised by his pin-point accurate striking, as well as his incredible athletic ability. He knocks out opponents with text book finesse, almost making it look easy. Described as an intelligent fighter, Alister incorporates only the best and most scientifically proven means to increase his rate of victory.

Recognising Wim Hof from his numerous super-human feats as well as numerous Guinness World Record titles, Alister began working with Wim Hof in order to increase his performance whilst competing.

From the moment they began working together, Alister witnessed an immediate increase in performance. Wim Hof, himself a native of the Netherlands, described Alister as 'An Intelligent Guy', crediting him as being a consummate professional when it came down to preparation for victory.

The method, however, is not confined to professionals such as Alister, it is for everyone. It has universal value across all sports bringing into alignment multiple physiological and mental attributes. More elite level athletes are beginning to recognise the mass benefits that come from using the method both in training and during competition.

Interpretation

For years, Wim Hof broke multiple endurance and physical stamina records, featuring in the Guinness Book of Records for some of the most super-human feats known to man. During this period, he was labelled as a genetic freak, pre-disposed to a type of physical gift.

The world was in awe of his power to withstand extremes of cold whilst exhibiting completely normal vital signs.

Scientists had never known such an enormous capacity to endure physical pressure and come out unscathed. Described as jolly, even ecstatic after completing such feats, he was, to most, a mystery to behold.

Upon further scientific enquiry involving a multitude of tests, Wim Hof demonstrated the immense untapped physical potential of the human body.

The real revelation came when he claimed he could teach anyone to perform to the same level as him using the simple method we have been discussing, later coined "The Wim Hof Method".

Conclusion

Any athlete across any sport will gain a more than considerable advantage from using this method and practicing it.

The advantages are various and manifold.

Heightened mental focus and drive to condition the cardiovascular system to work and perform at a much greater level of efficiency utilising brown fat for increased energy production and output.

Stimulation of the hormonal system, including increased levels of human growth hormone and testosterone, as well as the ability to access adrenaline whilst performing and competing.

Increased levels of stamina and endurance, resulting from ice baths. This conditions the body to withstand and cope with physical and mental stress whilst training and competing. It also works by increasing the body's capacity to take in and store oxygen naturally, producing greater physical and mental output.

Greater levels of restful deep sleep, generating increased recoverability between training and competing.

All of the above is made possible by dedicating as little as thirty minutes a day to practicing the fixed breathing cycle.

The Wim Hof Method enables anyone dedicated to the task, to become the "gifted" athlete they wish to be within their chosen sport. You too can perform as Wim Hof did himself when he entered the record books and took the world by storm.

CHAPTER TWO

Water and Coffee Enema

IN TODAY'S INDUSTRIAL WORLD, the human body is exposed to a mass of toxins that were not around until relatively recently.

For millennia, mankind lived in harmony with the environment with little or no exposure to anything toxic to the human body. Over the last 150 years, however, man has accelerated. The world, as a result, has changed in response, as science continues to evolve at a stellar rate…

This is of enormous benefit, taking mankind from the status of cave dweller and inhabitant of the jungles, into the modernity in just a few short leaps.

This remarkable shift comes with a huge trade off, however. The human body nowadays is exposed to a mass of toxins matching no other point in the history of the planet.

The toxins of today, come as a result of our huge industrial output which services us with all our physical needs from the water we drink, the food we eat and the products we manufacture, enabling toxins to find their way into our systems by way of a host of miscellaneous sources.

Regardless of the source, one immutable fact remains: When the human body is exposed to toxins it is our liver that is forced to deal with them doing its utmost to process and mitigate their harmful effects on our bodies.

The liver, therefore, is KEY to our survival. Understanding its fundamental role is essential to our fostering peak performance.

The Role of the Liver

In the first two minutes of reading this chapter, your liver has cleansed the entire quantity of blood flowing through your system, filtering out any toxins, retaining and processing in order for them to be excreted from your body through the bowels and into your toilet. If you stop to think about this, you will realise how incredible it it.

Your liver is also the king of energy production, storing up energy and essential nutrients required for the entire body to function properly. It could be accurately described as 'the engine of the human body'.

As the liver is the high performer within the body, it is essential that we make it a priority of concern in our quest to deliver an elite-level peak performance, providing it with everything it needs to increase and maintain its potency.

Nutrition, of course, is a crucial component when it comes to optimising the liver, namely when it comes to the consumption of cruciferous vegetables containing glutothimine, known to boost liver vitality.

Nutrition, however, constitutes only 50% of the equation when it comes to optimising the liver for delivering elite level peak performance. As described earlier, mankind today is exposed to a massive range of toxins.

These can be found in the water supply, food production, and manufacturing, as well as in other sources such as deodorants, aftershaves/perfumes, and household cleaning products, in certain types of clothing and even, perhaps most crucially, in the air we breathe.

Without the aid of the liver's powerful cleansing mechanism, these toxins would in time accumulate within the body leading to harm and disease.

The liver, however, still protects and fosters health within the body in spite of the multitude of toxins out there, in our environment today.

Optimising the Liver for Maximum Performance in Sport

The human body uses what is known as "The Process of Elimination" when it comes to removing toxins from within the body.

The pathways for this process entail breathing, sweating and the evacuation of faeces when we use the bathroom. With regards to the liver, the main pathway is, as mentioned earlier, the colon. It is of particular importance that attention is placed upon this elimination pathway.

History of the Enema

In World War 2, German soldiers were brought in from the battlefield after being injured.

The rate of casualties was high, and surgeons scrambled to save lives and limbs. In the chaos of the battlefield, they concluded that they did not have the adequate amount of morphine required to treat the mounting casualty rate.

In a desperate move, one of the surgeons had a 'eureka' moment. They had an ample stock of coffee that had been keeping them going through the night so he decided to fill an enema bag with coffee and administer it to one of the severely injured soldiers.

To the astonishment of the rest of his team, they witnessed the soldier undergoing instant pain relief. At a great rate, they began ministering coffee enemas to injured soldiers, with great success.

The coffee enema was born.

Science behind the Coffee Enema

Dr Max Gerson, pioneer of The Gerson Therapy performed extensive research into the human body. Described as Nutritional Therapy and used for the treatment of cancer and other diseases, the combination of drinking freshly blended juice alongside the daily practice of the coffee enema is the core foundation of The Gerson therapy.

Live enzymes contained within the fresh juice are absorbed into the body and serve as a type of police force, actively going to work on the source of the particular disease, breaking down tumours and other harmful disorders.

In simple terms, this could be likened to a physiological battle within the body. Toxins are broken down, waste material is carried in the blood system to the liver for processing, moving to evacuation via the colon, to ending up in the toilet as processed waste.

The consumption of live enzymes via the drinking of fresh juice could accurately be described as only 50% of The Gerson Therapy.

But what about the fallout waste material produced? And how does the coffee enema facilitate the removal of waste and toxins held within the liver?

Here is how and why the coffee enema works to form the other 50% of the therapy…

The Coffee Enema Explained

Coffee contains caffeine, which is a stimulant.

When room temperature coffee enters the colon via the enema route, the caffeine is absorbed through the hemorrhoidal veins. This travels via the portal vein to the liver. On arriving at the liver, the caffeine causes the bile ducts within the liver to relax.

This relaxing enables the liver to release its toxic load through the bowels and into the colon. Here, the waste, along with the fluid from the coffee mixture, can be expelled into the toilet.

The most important and significant consideration when performing a coffee enema, is the retaining of the coffee mixture in the colon for ten minutes.

This was formulated by Dr Gerson, as the optimum amount of time for the liver to cleanse itself of toxins.

As mentioned earlier, the liver cleanses the entire blood system every two minutes. Holding the coffee mixture, therefore, within the colon for ten minutes assists the liver to cleanse the blood five times over.

This could be described as a form of blood dialysis, further cleansing the body and promoting health.

The other important aspect of performing a correct coffee enema, is the ratio of coffee to water used to create the mixture.

For optimal results, take two tablespoons of caffeinated coffee (preferably organic).

Add to a saucepan and pour in two litres of still (also known as distilled) water.

Bring to the boil and allow to simmer for ten minutes. Allow to cool until lukewarm or room temperature.

You now have your coffee enema mixture.

All that is required now, is the purchase of an enema kit.

These can be purchased online for approximately $10. Most hold two litres, and come in various shapes and materials.

Purchasing "Medical Grade" kits will ensure you have one made from quality, non-perishable materials that can be reused over a long period.

Generally, the kits come with two nozzles – a long curved one, and a short two inch straight nozzle. We require only the short, two inch to perform the enema.

The tubing comes with either a small plastic tap, or small compression peg in order to control/stem the fluid from the enema bag as required.

You need to ensure that you are able to easily fill the enema bag, to control/stem the flow of fluid as required and that the unit holds the fluid without any risk of leakage.

How to Perform the Coffee Enema

Step 1

Place a large towel on to the floor or in a bath tub, as you prefer. Attach your enema bag to a fixed point approximately 1.5 metres above your towel, ensuring the enema tube is tangle free and that the tap/clip on the tube is in the CLOSED position.

Step 2

Fill the enema bag with your distilled water and organic coffee mixture, ensuring the mixture is no more than lukewarm/room temperature and NOT hot or cold.

Step 3

Lay down on your towel on your back. Make sure that you are able to easily access the enema tube, as well as access the tap/clip. Again, ensure the tube is tangle free.

Step 4

Now, holding the enema tube at the tap/clip with your left hand, turn and lay on your right side in a relaxed position. With your left hand, take the short nozzle at the end of the enema tube and insert into the anus approximately two to three inches. Ensure the short nozzle is stable and not able to easily slip out. It should feel comfortable.

Step 5

Now, relax, and with your left hand turn the tap/clip into the open position. All you have to do is lay comfortably whilst the mixture slowly enters the colon. If, for any reason, you experience mild wind or discomfort, simply pinch the enema tube to stem the flow and pause for a few moments until this discomfort passes. Release the pinch, allowing the mixture to flow again.

Continue and repeat as required until the contents of the enema bag are empty. Carefully, remove the nozzle from anus.

Step 6

Now that you have the mixture within your colon, relax and attempt to reach the recommended ten-minute time frame as explained earlier. If you are unable to achieve this, however, and are compelled to evacuate the colon prematurely, then please do so as necessary.

Next time however, try to gradually increase the amount of time you are able to hold the mixture until you achieve the magic number of ten minutes.

Congratulations – you did it!

You now feel fantastic, lighter, faster, clearer and minus any of the toxins held within your liver and body. Well done!

Coffee Enema Case Study

Ian Tudor is an expert on health and physical performance and the author of several bestselling books on Amazon, including Go! One Man's Guide to Health Vitality and Fat Loss.

Alongside his YouTube channel, Ian consults with a variety of athletes on finding new and innovative ways to increase their performance fast, incorporating only the best tried and tested methods to produce rapid results.

Researching and testing performance enhancement methods is never a work complete. It is an on-going quest to further test, innovate and refine what works for the elite athlete.

The majority of health gurus and coaches are quick to offer advice and guidance to athletes in order to increase performance. They have seldom tried and tested their own methods, however, and an increasing number hold only textbook-style theoretical diplomas without ever practicing their own theories.

Many shared classroom theories provide little or no differential advantage from conventional thinking. What Ian Tudor does, on the other hand, is provide a powerful game changing methodology obtained from the best sources. His methods have been personally tested and refined to ensure maximum advantage to elite athlete.

In short, Ian practices what he preaches!

Ian is a former gymnast for the city of Liverpool in addition to having a background in athletics and body-building. This means he has a clear understanding of exactly what works in delivering an elite level peak performance.

Upon studying the work of Dr Max Gerson, Ian began using the coffee enema protocol to gauge its merits as a performance enhancement tool.

The practice of performing a coffee enema produced multiple advantages with significant results.

Advantages

Coffee enemas cleanse the liver of toxins freeing up its capacity for energy production. Following his enema, Ian was instantly able to perform harder and longer in both cardio and load-bearing exercise.

It removes between five to ten pounds of processed waste from the colon instantly, making Ian pound for pound stronger and faster.

It serves as a means of stress release, creating an instant state of wellbeing and mental clarity.

Interpretation

The extensive research carried out by Dr Max Gerson was both unique and ground breaking.

Honing and refining his methodology on scores of patients, Gerson's focus and attention to detail made him a pioneer in the field of healing the body of disease.

His method was based around using the body's own capacity to eliminate toxins.

To Conclude

As an elite athlete, enabling the body to work as efficiently as possible is fundamental to peak performance in any sport, especially those requiring strength, speed, stamina and endurance.

The coffee enema protocol delivers on all of the above and provides the additional bonus of increased powers of recovery by vanquishing the body of waste materials accumulated from intense training and competition, whilst also bringing crystal clear mental focus.

What particularly stands out with this practice is that it is incredibly time and labour efficient. The enema kit can be taken and used anywhere, and the ten minutes it takes to perform, adds even further value to the practice.

In short, an athlete using this method has a distinct advantage over and above the athlete who does not!

A theoretical example could be the twin brother scenario.

TWIN BROTHER THEORY

Hypothetically, let's look at two identical twin brothers, both competitive boxers.

Each twin possesses the exact same attributes; physically and mentally. They have fought in ten boxing match bouts, and on every occasion the match has been a draw.

Before their eleventh bout, however, twin A undertakes a coffee enema.

The bout begins, and immediately twin A quickly moves across the ring landing an impressive uppercut. This is because, as he has zero waste in his colon due to the coffee enema, he is pound for pound stronger and quicker than twin B.

As the bout moves into the mid rounds, twin B is markedly more sluggish moving around the ring as twin A continues to land blows. The match continues, however, as both men possess the same level of skill.

Moving into the latter rounds twin A, by now is significantly faster, beating twin B to the punch in each exchange. This is because his liver is able to deliver much greater energy output as a result of the coffee enema, culminating in him being relatively fresh in comparison to the laboured movements of twin B.

Finally, in Round Eight, twin A lands a decisive blow to twin B and the referee declares a halt to the bout declaring twin A the winner of the match.

This example is, of course, theoretical.

It clearly demonstrates, however, how the same example can be applied across almost all sports. It illustrates the highly significant role that the liver plays in energy production, as well as the beneficial effect that the removal of five to ten pounds of processed dead weight from the colon has on increasing performance.

Another noteworthy element is that the enema facilitates the removal of parasites from the colon, which needlessly live on waste material as well as sapping energy and nutrients from the body. When this small parasitic ecosystem is removed, the body is able to consume less food deriving the same nutritional benefit. In addition, the food can be absorbed more efficiently.

CHAPTER THREE

Juicing

JUICING IS THE QUICKEST and most efficient way of getting vitamins and minerals into the body.

Studies concludes that when an individual begins juicing daily, a significant increase in physical performance and health is almost instantly observed. Whether it is someone suffering with an illness or health condition, or an elite athlete, the results are invariably the same.

1. Increased energy levels
2. Increased vitality
3. Increased performance

The reason for this is simple. When fruit and vegetable matter is broken down into a juice, the fibre is removed. This enables the body to fully access the nutrient content, quickly and easily, without having the burden of breaking down the fibre in the stomach.

By juicing, you are, essentially, bypassing this burden and allowing the juicer to perform the hard work of the body's digestion. Drinking a blended, nutrient-dense liquid that the body can easily absorb and utilise with ease, means that your own vital energy is conserved, and you are not bogging down the digestive system, with unnecessary amounts of fibre.

There is an important point to note here: Contained within a typical juice there could be a total of five carrots, five celery sticks, one green apple, and one lemon.

If you attempted to consume this amount of fruit and vegetables by eating them whole, you would need a significantly large amount of time, firstly to chew, and secondly to digest. This is on top of wasting the body's own finite vital energy by processing the mass.

When you consume a freshly blended juice, you are ingesting living enzymes that seek to clear out and actively keep the body in an optimum state of health. What is then clear is that there is no food or supplement that can supersede the immense nutritional value of consuming a freshly blended juice.

Let us take a closer look at the individual ingredients of a typical juice as mentioned above, and discover what they deliver.

1. Carrot

Carrots contain carotene.

Carotene is highly beneficial to the skin, giving you a healthy clear complexion. In addition, they are an excellent liver detoxifier. There are recorded examples of individuals with severely damaged livers, given only weeks to live, who made almost complete reversals of their diagnosis by doing nothing more than drinking fresh carrot juice.

As the liver is KING when it comes to energy production, as well as cleansing the blood, juiced carrots are a potent force.

2. Celery

Celery is excellent for providing an alkaline base which further helps to reduce inflammation in the body. It contains cells which increase and promote muscle flexibility. It also has a calming effect on the central nervous system. In short, celery is highly beneficial for athletic performance.

3. Green Apple

Green apples are a fantastic addition to juice because they contains pectins. Pectins have been proven to significantly reduce risk of cancer and other diseases. As seen in The Gerson Therapy – the nutritional programme for cancer and other diseases, green apple juice forms a vital ingredient in assisting in the reduction of tumours in cancer patients as well as being another excellent detoxifier.

4. Lemon

Lemon is unique in terms of its high potency as well as its beneficial effect on the body. Although lemons are acidic, they have an alkalising effect upon the liver. They help the liver to process toxins, which in turn frees up more of the liver's capacity for energy production, as well as a wide range of other essential functions. As a bonus, lemons are also packed with vitamin C.

So, you can see – the simple practice of consuming at least one juice a day will super-charge your ability to function and perform at a high level. Juicing provides the body with living enzymes, vitamins and minerals that it would struggle to gain from supplementation or other food sources alone.

This is purely down to the fact that consuming a vibrant, living source of nutrition such as a fresh juice beats all supplements and food sources. Drinking juice is far superior to consuming 'dead' foods such as off-the-shelf supplements; meat, tinned or packaged foods. Even though supplement manufacturers produce products which contain long extensive lists of beneficial ingredients, for the most part these are not absorbed or utilised usefully by the body. As stated above, the food is 'dead' and not in its natural living form. Instead, you will be consuming man-made, processed supplements that contain no more than a checklist of ingredients. They will be made with little or no consideration for how or why they are combined, or their effects on the body. The only real manufacturing considerations here are flavour, shelf life and profit margins!

Juice Guidelines

1. Purchasing a Juicer

So, you have decided to purchase a juicer. What should you look for?

Ideally, you should purchase a juicer which removes ALL of the fibre, as opposed to some models which allow some fibre to remain. Blenders are not recommended here as they will not extract the nutrients as purely and efficiently as juicers for optimal health. You will probably need to spend between $50 to $100 upwards for a juicer for everyday use.

2. The Effective Way to Consume Juice

Juicing is simple and straightforward. There are, however, a few important issues to note.

As outlined previously, fresh juice contains living enzymes which are highly beneficial. It is important to consume fresh juice immediately at room temperature. This is because studies have shown that refrigeration or leaving the juice in storage, significantly reduces its nutritional value. This directly reduces the "live" element of the juice.

In short, juice should be consumed IMMEDIATELY upon production.

3. Optimum time to consume Juice

It is essential that you have a clear understanding of the following:

The optimum time to consume specific nutrition,

alongside the knowledge of exactly what to consume. In this case, fresh juice.

Whenever, in your day, you choose to consume your juice will have a significant role in how much of the nutrients your body can uptake and use, as opposed to being excreted through the process of urination.

In order to gain maximum nutrition from your juice, you have several options. All of these work on the same physiological basis, which is ensuring maximum uptake of nutrients.

The principle to be aware of here, is one of depletion. This means being in a slightly fasted state, or at the very least, a depleted state such as early in the morning. This will ensure your body is hungry for simple sugars. You have several options to achieve this window of opportunity before you consume the juice.

1. First thing upon rising, on an empty stomach. This ensures you are in a fasted state from a full night's sleep.

2. Immediately after cardio or other physical type training, when you are in a calorie deficit, again similar to above.

3. Immediately after competition, or a phase of competition, whereby you are not required to compete again for several hours. Again, physiologically similar to the method above.

The basic premise with the above three methods is this:

When your body is in a depleted state, such as when

glycogen stores have been utilised in the muscles, your body has a greater propensity or incentive to pull up and store as much of the consumed nutrition within this golden window of opportunity. In this case, a highly nutritious fresh juice. This process of depletion, followed by the uptake of nutrients afterwards, could be likened to fully pushing down on a syringe in order to allow it maximum capacity to draw up the largest amount of nutrition available.

Of course, I have put this very simply for the purposes of illustration. There are multiple numbers of physiological processes at work. It is not, however, necessary to describe each of these in detail, as this additional knowledge would be surplus to the purpose of this book which is about to producing peak athletic performance.

Juicing Case Study

Brian Pace, author of 'Juicing for Athletes,' as well as many other sports related books, cites juicing as being fundamental in in the ability to increase an elite level athletes performance.

Brian began his sports career as an elite level table tennis star. Competing for the U.S. Olympic team, he later went on to become an elite-level mountain bike competitor and cyclist racer. These disciplines led him to becoming an elite coach, as well as nutritional coach of other high level sports competitors, sharing over twenty eight years of knowledge and wisdom gleaned from being at the high end of Olympic and nutritional coaching.

Brian is known for stating that, "An athlete's performance is increased within their own kitchen…"

This is a benchmark statement that Brian uses to emphasise the huge role proper nutrition plays in increasing physical performance.

Interpretation

Juicing is widely recognised as a superior way to nourish the body, as well as elicit peak athletic performance. From Olympic athletes to individuals with medical conditions, juicing increases and maintains the health and vitality of the body more effectively than any supplement or food source.

To Conclude

As a serious elite level athlete, you must incorporate juicing into your regime in order to ensure peak performance in both training and competition. As well as juicing daily, you must also attempt to consume fresh juice whilst your body is in a deficit state, as explained in "Juicing Guidelines," thereby maximising the amount of nutrients pulled into your body.

Remember to maintain this two-pronged approach daily.

Firstly, juicing, and secondly, consuming your juice within a deficit state.

If you do this, your peak performance is more or less guaranteed!

CHAPTER FOUR

Earthing

WE LIVE IN A HIGHLY TECHNOLOGICAL AGE and we are surrounded by energy in the form of microwaves from Wi-fi outlets and cell towers, alongside EMF waves coming at us from a whole host of other wireless devices.

This energy is a feature of our modern lives. As human beings, however, our bodies have only been exposed to this level of exposure for less than two decades. Already within this short period, studies have clearly shown that such exposure can have real health consequences in terms of affecting our body.

Sleep disorders and mood disturbances such as anxiety and depression are linked to the current levels of energy all around us, absorbed into our body through the skin and into our blood. Some have described this as a type of "charging" of our bodies. Certainly, the numerous studies carried out around this subject would suggest this as an accurate description. The good news is that new cutting edge studies into a process known as "Earthing" have conclusively revealed that we can discharge these large amounts of energy from our body by simply connecting our bodies with earth. Furthermore, by doing so, we can unlock a whole host of additional health and physical performance benefits.

Before we explore the raft of benefits let me first explain the science behind Earthing and exactly how it works.

Science Behind Earthing

In its most simple form, Earthing is about making direct physical contact between our bodies and the earth in order to discharge positively charged electrons from our bodies. This also negatively charges the electrons in our body, causing a stabilising effect on the electrical system within us.

This can be achieved by simply walking around or standing bare foot on the ground outdoors once daily for five minutes or more.

The real discovery from the twenty-one scientifically verified studies into Earthing is that our bodies have evolved over millennia to work in unison and harmony with the negatively charged electrical field of the earth. The issue is that since the 1960's when we began wearing synthetic soles on our feet, our bodies have become completely insulated from the powerful benefits of the electrical rejuvenating field of the earth. This means that for the most part, our insulated bodies are becoming more and more inflamed due to this crucial, yet neglected, part of our physiology.

Our bodies operates on an electrical system. From our heart to our lungs to our brain. Logic, therefore, would lead us to the conclusion that when this intricate system is disturbed by external electrical waves in the environment, the system moves out of alignment. This creates imbalances within the body such as the aforementioned sleep disturbances and/or depression or anxiety.

The solution of course is Earthing our body to foster balance to the body's electrical system.

Now that we have a general understanding of the science behind Earthing, let us cover the host of additional performance enhancing benefits of Earthing derived from the previously mentioned twenty-one verified studies.

Performance Enhancing Benefits of Earthing

In one study, test subject blood samples were taken before and after Earthing.

All the test results were identical, in that the blood cells taken before the subjects were Earthed showed blood cells as being very close together and constricted. When, however, the blood samples taken after the subjects had been Earthed were examined, the blood cells were significantly further apart. This demonstrated a more relaxed appearance and better level of viscosity associated with an improvement in health.

People within another control group showed a marked increase in their immune system after Earthing for just a few days, alongside far deeper sleep patterns.

Another group of older test subjects, aged between sixty and seventy years of age, all suffering from inflammatory and auto immune conditions such as Arthritis, Multiple Sclerosis and Fibromyalgia reported a massive reduction in pain and inflammation after Earthing following just a few days. Some exhibited zero amounts of pain, so much so, they were able to withdraw from the multiple pain medications that had dogged their quality of life for years.

A test group of athletes split into two distinct groups: One Earthed, the other not Earthed.

After performing the same exercises, the Earthed group demonstrated a far higher resistance to muscle pain when both groups were tested. Some initial scientific studies are now proving that Earthing has a pronounced and highly beneficial effect directly on the organ systems of the body, healing and strengthening these systems.

This lead to a further study performed on injured athletes, sleeping on an Earthing mat. The athletes witnessed far greater levels of recovery in terms of the duration of a specific injury having Earthed. Other studies have clearly shown Earthing to have a profound stabilising effect on irregular hormonal rhythms. Conditions such as PMS, for example, reduced dramatically after just a short amount of Earthing.

The conclusion of these multiple, verified studies is that Earthing is scientifically proven to not only work but to be hugely beneficial to health and injury recovery, as well as facilitating peak athletic performance.

Earthing Guidelines

In order to maximise the immense benefit earthing has on peak performance, we shall explore some of the most effective methods for Earthing. We will also cover some of the products currently on the market that can be used to increase the amount of time during the day and night that we are connected to Earth.

1. The Classic Method

The Classic Method is to simply walk or stand upon the ground bare foot each day for a minimum of five minutes. This could also include lying on the ground bare foot wearing non-synthetic clothing such as cotton.

This method alone, performed daily, is hugely beneficial to health. The important thing to bear in mind is to ensure you stand or lay on level grass, soil or some other naturally conductive material, not asphalt or certain other man-made materials such as rubber or plastic.

An excellent method for Earthing for anyone who trains outdoors, is to simply lay on a patch of grass after session for a five-minute period. This method is as good as any product on the market and costs nothing other than five minutes of your time.

2. The Earthing Mat

The Earthing mat is becoming more and more popular for busy individuals who, for whatever reason, do not have the time or regular access to a patch of level Earth. This could be due to living in a large city, a high rise building perhaps or working in such a building.

The mat works by being connected to a cable. At one end of the cable is a plug prong that fits directly into the earthed component in a standard electrical outlet. Depending on what country you live, the plug you receive will vary. This connects the mat with the earthing system of whichever particular building you are in.

As long as your skin makes direct contact with the mat, you are Earthed. Also, you can test whether your mat is properly earthed by either purchasing a cheap earthing meter, or by asking an electrician to test the mat with an electrical testing tool.

These mats come in various sizes and each have a specific application. There is, for example, an earthing mat used for sleeping on, a mat you stand bare foot on, as well as a mouse mat designed for someone working in an office or an environment with computers. One or more of these products is no better or worse than the other, rather, each is geared towards the particular criteria or lifestyle of the individual purchasing the mat.

3. Other Earthing Products

Working on the same principle of connecting to the earth component of an electrical outlet, are some other products to consider that may also be of value depending on your specific requirements.

Bedding products such as quilt covers, mattress covers, pillow covers and blankets are the newer lines of earthing products to come on to the market. These are generally more expensive due to a more intricate manufacturing process and some contain more expensive conductive material such as silver. The benefits of being earthed whilst sleeping are various and manifold as already mentioned above. The fundamental drawback with any of these bedding products is primarily cost, followed by durability. When combining a fine conductive material within a fabric that requires regular cleaning, the conductivity and effectiveness of these products can diminish over time.

Some other cost-effective earthing products to consider are earthing socks and the wearable earthing wrist band, another excellent product that can be worn during the daytime whilst at home or at work or overnight.

Earthing Case Study

During the Tour de France, one of the competitors, Pablov, suffered a serious injury. It had the potential to end his participation within the competition. Upon treating him, however, the decision was taken to further treat the injury with an Earthing pad.

That evening Pablov slept with the Earthing pad connected to his injury. The next morning, after enjoying an undisturbed night, the injury was inspected in order to determine whether he would be permitted to continue the Tour.

The examination declared him fit to continue. His astonishing overnight recovery from a serious injury was directly attributed to the use of the Earthing pad, that had been applied directly to the injury.

The Earthing technology has proved so groundbreaking that it has now been used in the treatment of injuries of multiple competitors in the Tour de France. Great results have come about on treating and healing injuries sustained whilst competing in one of the most gruelling races on the planet. The Earthing technology has made such a difference to competitors in the Tour de France that coaches and physiotherapists, have made it standard practice for all athletes competing in the race to be earthed at night. They recognise unequivocally that Earthing technology plays a pivotal role in rest and recovery as well as for the treatment of injury. The competitors themselves realise the depth of restful sleep they receive when earthed at night.

Interpretation

Earthing was a treatment for the human body, was conceptualised by Clint Ober in 1999 in the United States.

Ober began testing the idea using standard electrical duct tape on his bed. He attached this to a cable that was connected to a grounding rod placed into the ground outside. He experienced an immediate result by having a good night's sleep.

A short time later he approached UCLA and asked if they would consider conducting a study into the theory of Earthing on one's health. The UCLA promptly dismissed his request as something close to a joke.

Undeterred, Clint began his own study, using fifty test subjects with medical conditions, ranging from MS, Arthritis and other inflammatory conditions each leading to severe pain.

The study was simple. Its aim was to discover whether earthing the fifty test subjects made any measurable difference to their pain levels.

His findings of the first pioneering study could not be ignored.

The test subjects ALL described a dramatic decrease in pain, as well as being able to get a restful night's sleep.

Physicists, medical doctors, and surgeons suddenly took notice of this new field of discovery especially, as the studies continued proving the numerous sceptics, wrong. The over-riding conclusion was that Earthing is essential for health, essential for wellbeing and of course essential for peak performance.

To Conclude

As an elite athlete, you should incorporate Earthing into your daily regime.

As shown above, there are a multitude of products of immense value depending on your schedule as well as geographical location.

There are two key areas of Earthing.

The first priority is to ensure that you are Earthed while asleep at night. This is proven to be incredibly beneficial across all of studies. How you achieve this Earthing is a matter of personal choice. New products are coming on to the market all the time. There are even free instructional videos online that show you how to make your own Earthing equipment for the more hands-on and adventurous athletes among us!

Secondly, connect to earth during the daytime for a minimum of five minutes, and up to twenty minutes if possible. This can either be bare foot or simply sitting on the ground whilst bare foot.

CHAPTER FIVE

Meditation

MEDITATION IS BY FAR THE SINGLE MOST beneficial performance enhancer for any athlete wishing to compete at an elite level and deliver at peak performance.

It enables an individual to transcend both physical and psychological limitations bringing together mind and body, to supersede the efforts of other competitors who may use the exact same training methods and consume the same level of nutrition, yet do not meditate.

You may be asking yourself right now – how could this be possible?

Let me explain why…

How Meditation Works

Surrounding us, energy vibrates at a certain frequency. What we perceive as solid and fixed is actually vibrating on a sub-atomic level. This includes every particle in our bodies. Any physicist will confirm that when matter is examined at a sub-atomic level, what is observed is energy expressing its form in accordance with a particular vibrational frequency.

You can attribute this to whatsoever you wish. The Universe, God or another spiritual higher power… the fact remains unchanged. Namely that all around us, as well as within us, energy is expressing itself by means of a vibrational frequency.

This being established scientifically – where does meditation come into the universal equation?

When an individual meditates, they are esentially bringing every particle in their body into alignment with the surrounding vibrational frequency of the universe. They become as one with the energy all around them, harmonising on a sub atomic level as opposed to being out of synchronicity.

Depending upon your own personal background and level of understanding, this concept may or may not seem far out and abstract. Any physicist will confirm this to be an accurate, albeit basic explanation of energy and the role it plays within the universe. When we meditate we are literally communing with the very essence of the Universe. Namely the universal force that creates and drives all things. When we develop this connection, we experience the divine, a oneness that can only be fully appreciated by the meditation practitioner. This experi- ence of oneness is best encountered personally, Attempting to *describe* it, is secondary to *feeling* it for yourself.

Now we have explained the role meditation plays, let us go into how it increases performance and how it affects the body. I will start with the science behind meditation.

Science Behind Meditation

1. Energy alignment – Meditation brings every particle in the body into alignment with the vibrational force of the surrounding universe, bringing the body into harmony.

2. Practicing meditation daily builds up the frontal parts of the brain. These are the parts responsible for decision making and perception, increasing the capacity to make better decisions as well as an increased level of perception.

3. Cholesterol contained within the blood is reduced significantly, as meditating serves in cleansing the blood and allowing it to flow more freely. This in turn significantly reduces stress hormones and cortisol levels in the blood.

4. Cell Production
Meditation causes the liver to produce new healthy cells, facilitating greater recovery and performance.

5. Increased Cardiovascular performance and energy output
As meditation is a monitoring of breath, it naturally increases the efficiency of the cardiovascular system, increasing the ability to get in to the zone and perform at a high level. This is because the practice of meditation creates a deep neural connection between the brain and the cardiovascular system.

6. Greater powers of recovery

Meditation forges deep neurological pathways within the brain. Over time, these new neural pathways facilitate in contributing to greater powers of recovery both during competition and between training sessions. This enables you to bounce back far quicker than athletes who do not practice meditation.

The History of Meditation

Meditation has its roots in the ancient religious and spiritual practices of our ancestors. From Tibetan Monks to the Indian Yogis and the early Christians and Jews, practicing meditation was done as a means to bring about greater mindfulness and spirituality. These ancient peoples only had a limited concept of the beneficial power of meditation on physical health, so most meditated as a means to worship their particular God.

The Miracle of Meditation

A miracle is defined as a thing that transcends human understanding. The practice of meditation can be defined as one such miracle. Scientists do not understand how it works, they simply know that it does.

Numerous verified studies confirm that meditation enhances a practitioner's physiology on a cellular level. Examples of this can be found in the modern Indian Yogis, able to perform the most extraordinary feats of human strength by lifting ten times their own bodyweight, to Tibetan Monks who can withstand being cocooned in ice cold sheets for twenty-four hours whilst maintaining completely normal vital signs as well as core temperature.

These are just two examples of countless other verifiable scientific studies conducted into the practice of meditation.

How to Meditate

1. Fix a set time each day when you will be undisturbed by people, phones and other disturbances. Take the time to explain to family members or colleagues that during this time you do not wish to be notified of anything that may require your attention.

2. To begin with, ten minutes is a reasonable amount of time to meditate. As you become more proficient you can gradually increase this time period. The use of a timer is recommended, as it can be used to log progress as you improve.

3. Find a place where you feel comfortable, with no loud noises or other distractions. Designate this as your meditation area. You can customise this area to be as pleasant as possible, using some additional cushions or pillows. You can meditate almost anywhere, so long as it is comfortable and distraction-free. You should also set aside some clothing that brings you into a relaxed state. This could be some soft cotton pyjamas or other natural material that puts you into a relaxed mood.

4. Now sitting comfortably, take in a deep breath. As you begin to exhale, allow the outward breath to make an

OHM sound. Imagine you are stretching out each outward breath as long as possible before taking in another deep breath, allowing the outward sound of OHM to clear and empty your mind. As you stretch out the outward breath, you make should be a long oooooooooh sound, which will conclude with the OHM. It is good to bear in mind that the OHM sound is simply a means to monitor your outward breath. Aim for a consistency of sound with each outward breath and allow your mind to clear with each exhale.

There is no wrong or right way to meditate, only minor variations in sound produced so do not feel discouraged if one day it does not work for you. Focus, instead, on getting your ten minutes each day and progress is certain.

What do I mean by progress?

Increased mental clarity, focus and concentration during the day, as well as an all over feeling of inner calm and wellbeing. There are no drawbacks to meditation, only advantages. You can become the 'calm in the storm' able to solve problems internally and externally when most around you are overwhelmed or immobilised by stress.

This incredible game changer is yours for the taking accessed through the daily practice of meditation.

Meditation Case Study

NBA superstar, LeBron James of the Los Angeles Lakers is often feted as the greatest basketball player in the world. Winner of four NBA Most Valuable Player Awards, two Olympic gold medals and three NBA Finals MVP Awards, he is at the top of his game.

He is also one of a growing number of elite athletes known to incorporate meditation into his intense physical training regime, a practise he cites as essential to his success.

For LeBron James, meditation is so vital to his physical wellbeing that not only does he meditate daily in the privacy of his own home, he has also been known to draw games to a halt in order to take meditation time-outs as a means of focusing his mind and reduce anxiety.

Where basketball is a high paced sport, what LeBron brings to each match is a sense of calm as if each every game is played in slow motion. He creates precision and accuracy taking his time with each shot and as a result produces rare brilliance that contrasts with the high pressured environment in which he plays.

Advantages

There is the belief that meditation is a mental practise that impacts only on the health of the mind but regular practitioners of the craft also extol its virtues as highly beneficial to the body.

Meditation aligns the mind with the body, reduces anxiety and creates an environment of calm before and after the intense physical stress of a high performance game.

By placing oneself into a state of stillness, calm and relaxation, meditation has also been proven to aid in recovery by creating an optimal state of wellbeing. In order to become skilled at meditation, however, one must mediate. It only improves with practise. By undertaking the process on a daily basis, it is possible for athletes to become highly effective at the craft and thus better able tro have it work for them.

Interpretation

Losing focus is a major issue for athletes, split second loss of concentration can cost them their game.

Being able to detach your mind from stress while at the same time visualising where you want to be and how to get there is key to success and one of the main factors that sets an elite athlete apart from his or her competitors.

Meditation, by calming the mind directly calms the body and allows you the space you need to focus on the task in hand.

To Conclude

Meditation is a vital practise for anyone with a busy life and busy schedule but for athletes looking to be the top of their game, it can be the difference between winning and losing, success and failure.

By being 'in the moment' but mentally apart from the stress of an intense situation game gives you the scope and foresight to view the game objectively and maintain the vital sense of calm.

CHAPTER SIX

Foods to Eliminate

IN ORDER TO ENABLE THE BODY to function and perform at its highest level, certain foods need to be eliminated from the diet.

These are specific types of food that have been proven to cause inflammation in the body, as well as disrupt bodily processes. During training or competing, the following foods should not be consumed. They can, however, be consumed moderately during holidays or festive periods.

1. Wheat or foods containing wheat

In 1970 Norman Borlock received the Nobel Prize for successfully increasing the amount of wheat that could be grown per square foot, four-fold. This was a huge leap forward in solving famine and other food crises across the world. This four-fold increase was groundbreaking for food producers.

It was achieved by altering the structure of the wheat on a cellular level. A type of acid was introduced to the wheat cells which caused a mutation. It was this muta-tion that increased the yield so significantly.

The wheat produced today is as a direct result of the

above method. In its natural form, wheat grows up to 6ft tall, whilst the modern modified wheat known as "Dwarf Wheat" grows only to knee height, thus producing considerably more per acre than in its original form.

In the New York best-selling book *The Wheat Belly* by Dr William Davis, the difficulty faced by the body when attempting to process modified wheat is dicussed in depth.

Its impact, firstly, on increased levels of body fat. When wheat is consumed, it dramatically raises blood triglycerides. One round of bread, for example, can have the same effect on blood sugar as consuming six teaspoons of white sugar. This is a startling statistic. In addition, wheat interferes with gut health. The gut houses 80% of the immune system, and overconsumption of wheat can lead to a condition known as "Leaky Gut" whereby protein leaks through the wall of the gut into the blood, causing inflammation.

This can manifest in joint pain, headaches, constipation, digestive issues including IBS, as well as mood disorders such as depression or anxiety.

Another standout feature of modern wheat is that it is addictive. An individual requires a period of seven days or more after ceasing to consume wheat before they feel the benefit. The effects on physical and mental performance is significant.

In short, eliminating wheat will pay dividends in terms of performance, as well as health.

An excellent substitute for wheat is rice. In fact, when this simple substitution is made, most find their digestive issues, joint pain, low mood, along with body fat disappears over the course of a few short weeks.

2. Processed Dairy including Milk

Dairy is produced today on a gargantuan scale. The methods used have been refined over the decades in order to produce the greatest yields possible, as processed food manufacturing has risen to meet the demands of consumers. Many of these newly produced processed foods require dairy as an ingredient, which in turn has ramped up demand.

Dairy in its natural form can be beneficial to health. The modern processing methods, however, are not conducive to increasing vitality within the body. Cows are made to produce milk far in excess of their normal cycle. This is achieved by keeping the animals constantly pregnant, using artificial insemination as a means to maintain their milk production. It is because of this and modern farming methods, that animals often become sick. To counteract sickness, the animals are given antibiotics, as well as other drugs. The end result is the production of more milk.

Milk produced, however, is of such a low standard, that if it were to be consumed at this stage it would likely cause sickness to the individual. It is for this reason that the milk is further processed, using what's known as pasteurisation, the process named after its founder French scientist Louis Pasteur. In this process, milk is heated to a high temperature and then cooled in order to kill harmful microbes contained within the milk. The mere fact that this process is even required indicates that this mass produced milk is not the most nutritious substance to consume. In fact, the pasteurisation process was originally intended for use with beer and wine production, not with milk.

As a result of these intensive manufacturing processes, milk causes issues for the body when consumed alongside its other derivatives such as cheese, yogurt, cream etc. Some of these issues include poor digestion, IBS, constipation, psoriasis, eczema, increased irritability, weakening of bones, as well as being known to increase the risk of fits and seizures to individuals with epilepsy.

Many nutritionalists have also cited dairy as a sugary substance that over time can deplete nutrients from the body as it is forced to work harder to excrete it from the body. In short it should not be consumed during training or competition as it detracts from the bodies' ability to perform at a high level.

An excellent substitute for processed milk/dairy is goats milk, which is nutrient dense and absorbed much more easily.

CHAPTER SEVEN

Standardisation and Sequencing

IN ORDER FOR YOU TO MAXIMISE YOUR PERFORMANCE, it is essential that you have a clear understanding of the role standardisation and proper sequencing play in putting you at the top of your game.

The methods and practices outlined previously in this book are each individually powerful. When standardised and sequenced, however, in the right order, they combine in delivering a force that will sky rocket your level of performance to new heights.

Let us start with Standardisation, and the important role it has on delivering peak performance.

Standardisation

Learning and understanding each individual practice in this book will yield incredible value in your quest to become the best athlete you can possibly be.

Although studying the best methods alone is not necessarily a guarantee of success, many athletes know or possess knowledge that is of course of great value. They fall into complacency, however, by becoming performance 'experts' instead of performance 'practitioners'…

In order for you to become the best, you must first

learn a particular method, and grasp it theoretically. Secondly, you must practice it again and again until your theoretical level of understanding matches your level of practical proficiency.

They say practice makes perfect, but what really makes perfect is perfect practice.

So, with this in mind, be sure to start with the first method and practice it whilst making small refinements as you go until you are both expert AND expert practitioner. Avoid moving on to the next method until you have completely nailed the first.

When you have achieved proficiency, it is important that you standardise the newly acquired skill into your daily routine so as to retain the skill, before moving on to the next, and so on and so forth. This is the very essence of standardisation.

An excellent technique you can use to lock in the particular practice is one used by student medical surgeons, namely, to learn the particular practice, perform the particular practice, then teach the practice to someone else.

This simple three-fold technique has a powerful psychological effect on locking in a skill and is easy to apply. It is the tried and tested method of professional surgeons that will work equally well for you in becoming the best athlete you can be.

Sequencing

The sequence, or order in which we do something, is the key to victory in sport. Olympic Gold Medalists know this to be the case…4th place and beyond runner up, perhaps not so well.

A correct sequencing of our newly acquired skills will set the stage for 1st place and serve to act as the springboard that elevates you over and above the competition.

Proper sequencing of the methods in this book will relate directly to your specific chosen sport. As this book is written as a guide for all elite level competitive athletes, it would be a huge undertaking to outline a sequence for every individual sport. This would not be in line with the intention and purpose of this book, which is namely to provide an elite athlete with a concise and easy to understand guide to peak performance.

Below I have, however, devised two sequences that would greatly serve the mainstay of professional athletes.

These are labeled sequence A and sequence B, featuring a short explanation for what each one is geared towards.

Sequence A

This is a sequence that is focused towards increasing all attributes, both physical and psychological, increasing energy within the body as well as sharpening and focusing the mind. It is an easy to implement, generalised sequence that will take you to a higher level of performance than you are currently at. The sequence can be done every day, and for most athletes will suffice in acting as the all-around game changer that will propel you to the top of your chosen sport.

1. Thirty minutes of meditation
2. Perform The Wim Hof Method, including a cold shower or ice bath for advanced practitioners
3. Consume a fresh juice using the recipe outlined in the juicing section
4. Earthing: Lie on a level patch of natural ground, preferably grass, on your back for ten to twenty minutes. This is an excellent time for your body to begin absorbing the nutrients from the juice.
5. Coffee Enema. With the nutrients and live enzymes from the juice working in your system, the next part of the equation is the removal of toxins from the liver and processed waste from the colon

Congratulations on completing your first sequence.

Sequence B

In sequence B, the focus is placed on competitive performance, and so this sequence is built around a specific sporting event. This is to serve only as an example, and so you should experiment during your training periods with formulating a unique sequence that is both optimal for your particular sport as well as being suited to you personally.

Again, this requires some experimentation and testing during training. At this stage, however, as will have gained experience and expertise in performing each of the methods laid out in this book, it should not be difficult for you to intrinsically know what type of sequence will naturally be advantageous to you whilst performing your chosen sport.

Sequence B should be viewed as a form of template that may be altered to serve you in both training and competition.

1. Thirty minutes of meditation upon rising
2. Consumption of a fresh juice

The next part of sequence B is built directly around training and competition. If, for example, your sport involves rounds, or short to medium time periods between performing, this can be ideal for bringing in the breathing component of the Wim Hof Method, which can be done in just a few minutes and will boost your next performance.

For slightly longer periods between performance, along with accessible privacy, the Coffee Enema can be employed. This works especially well for sports which are highly physically demanding and followed by medium to long break periods in between competing. It is important to be aware of the time each method requires. A total of three minutes for the breathing component of the Wim Hof Method, and fifteen to twenty minutes for the Coffee Enema.

3. The breathing component of the Wim Hof Method between sets or rounds of competition
4. The Coffee Enema for medium to longer periods between sets or rounds of competition, typically fifteen minutes or more, recommended no more than three in any one-day period.

5. Earthing. This is relatively simple to undertake and depends solely on your location. It can be undertaken by the removal of footwear and standing on natural ground between sets or rounds, or by the use of an earthing device connected to a nearby outlet.

Summary

Sequence A gives you a fixed template that will enhance your performance drastically and can be used daily before training or competing.

Sequence B is a specific sequence built around an athletes' particular sport, and so the components order should be decided upon by the athlete, with the main consideration being time constraints.

CHAPTER EIGHT

In Conclusion

'The Wise Man builds his house upon the rock...'

THE SOLE PURPOSE OF PRODUCING THIS BOOK is to demonstrate the importance of creating a solid foundation for any elite athlete capable of reaching peak performance.

Knowledge is power. In this modern era of technology, we are bombarded with information on an uncontrollable scale. This book aims to deliver the best and most relevant knowledge to you, the reader, without overwhelming you with mass information overload.

It is important to me that the book is short and concise while still delivering a powerful tool to your victory. The true challenge in writing, lies in creating an easy-to-understand format that any athlete can pick up and mentally digest, giving you the tools that you need to practice or employ in order to succeed. I have kept the book lean, removing convoluted or complicated information, technical or otherwise, that draws away from its intrinsic value to you.

I am satisfied that the book delivers what it has set out to accomplish, and I am incredibly proud of producing something both unique as well as magical blending the best of the best, from several fields of expertise, into one powerful little book.

I hope you have enjoyed reading this. My intention is that it continues to provide you with immense value within all your endeavours as an athlete as well as within your every day life.

Kindest Regards
Ian Tudor

***

If you have enjoyed reading this book, then please feel free to leave a review online. Once again, thank you for purchasing this book, and best regards.

www.ingramcontent.com/pod-product-compliance
Lightning Source LLC
Chambersburg PA
CBHW070335090426
42733CB00012B/2490